The GREAT BARRIER REEF

A LIVING LABORATORY

The GREAT BARRIER REEF

A LIVING LABORATORY

by Rebecca L. Johnson

Lerner Publications Company
Minneapolis

For my friends in Oz

Library of Congress Cataloging-in-Publication Data

Johnson, Rebecca L.
    The Great Barrier Reef: a living laboratory : by Rebecca L.
Johnson
        p. cm.
    Includes index.
    Summary: An account of various research projects involving
the animal and plant life of Australia's Great Barrier Reef.
    ISBN 0-8225-1596-2
    1. Coral reef biology—Queensland—Great Barrier Reef—
Juvenile literature. [1. Coral reef biology. 2. Great Barrier Reef
(Qld.)]
I. Title.
QH197.J64   1991
574.9943—dc20   91-10096
                                                          CIP
                                                           AC

Manufactured in the United States of America
1   2   3   4   5   6   7   8   9   10   99   98   97   96   95   94   93   92   91

Contents

These ribbon reefs are among the thousands of coral reefs that make up the Great Barrier Reef, which stretches for more than 1,300 miles along the northeastern coast of Australia.

6

"All aboard, ladies and gentlemen! The ferry will be leaving in five minutes!" the captain announces over the big ship's loudspeaker. The visitors begin making their way down the wooden dock jutting out from the beach, a gentle curve of golden sand that hugs one side of the narrow island.

At first glance, all the ferry passengers look like tourists. There are parents with sunburned children, a group of noisy teenagers, and several older couples wearing big straw hats to protect them against the hot Australian sun. Also in the group are two tanned young men with towels wrapped around their waists, covering their swimsuits. They are carrying scuba gear. As the people take their seats on the ferry, most are laughing and talking about their relaxing day in the sun. But the moment the two men sit down, they launch into a serious discussion.

"I'd say it will be next week, Russ," says one of the men. "I think so too, Peter," agrees his companion. "They're nearly ripe. I'd guess that they'll go off Thursday or Friday. Just after the full moon, as usual."

Who are these two men, and what are they talking about? Despite their casual appearance, they are not tourists. They are marine biologists Peter Harrison and Russ Babcock. All day long, while the other passengers were taking it easy, these two scientists have been hard at work. Using scuba gear, they have spent most of the day doing research underwater. Today they discovered that something they have been waiting for all year is about to take place. Not just here, around this tiny island, but all up and down Australia's Great Barrier Reef.

7

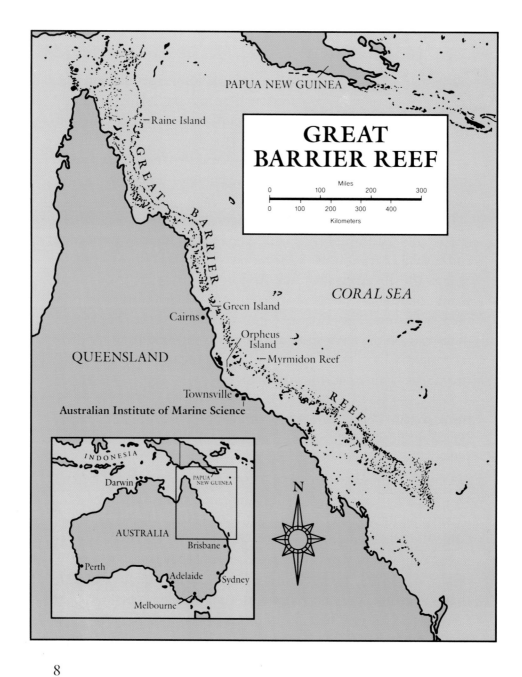

GREAT
BARRIER REEF

Miles
0 · 100 · 200 · 300

Kilometers
0 · 100 · 200 · 300 · 400

PAPUA NEW GUINEA

Raine Island

GREAT BARRIER REEF

Green Island

Cairns

Orpheus Island

Myrmidon Reef

CORAL SEA

QUEENSLAND

Townsville

Australian Institute of Marine Science

INDONESIA

Darwin

PAPUA NEW GUINEA

AUSTRALIA

Brisbane

Perth

Adelaide

Sydney

Melbourne

N

THE GREAT BARRIER REEF

A LIVING LABORATORY

The Great Barrier Reef is one of the earth's natural wonders. It stretches for nearly 1,300 miles (2,090 kilometers) along the northeastern coast of Australia. The reef is not a single formation, but a huge collection of many individual coral reefs (at least 2,600!). It is the largest group of coral reefs in the world. All together, the Great Barrier Reef covers an area about half the size of Texas.

Coral reefs are living structures built up over thousands of years by tiny animal architects called **polyps** (PAH-lips). Coral polyps are simple animals, cousins of jellyfish and sea anemones. The body of a polyp is little more than a tiny sack with a mouth at one end. Around the mouth is a ring of tentacles.

Coral polyps usually live together in groups, or colonies. Each polyp manufactures a stony skeleton around its body, and the skeletons of all the polyps in a colony are joined together. When the polyps die, their delicate bodies decay, but their hard skeletons remain behind. New polyps

9

Coral polyps with their tentacles extended. Polyps use their tentacles to catch and kill tiny animals in the water around them.

grow on top of the "bones" of their ancestors. Gradually, over long periods of time, huge masses, or **reefs**, of coral skeletons are built up in the ocean, with a layer of living corals on the surface.

Coral polyps make their living as predators. They use their tentacles, which are covered with stinging cells, to catch and kill microscopic animals that drift past in the water. But coral polyps also get food from another, very unusual, source. They have tiny, one-celled plants called **zooxanthellae** (zoh-zan-THEL-ee) living inside them. Zooxanthellae use sunlight to make food for themselves and their coral hosts. Because zooxanthellae need lots of sunlight to manufacture food, reef-building corals are found only in clear, shallow ocean waters.

Coral colonies come in all sorts of shapes and sizes and colors. On the reefs that make up the Great Barrier Reef, there are more than 350 different kinds of corals. But a coral reef is more than just a collection of corals. It is home to an astonishing variety of living things.

If you were to dive into the warm waters around a coral reef, what would you see? There would be tropical fish that sparkle like jewels, sponges, sea squirts, colorful marine worms, enormous anemones with waving tentacles. You would probably also see big blue starfish, spotted sea cucumbers, giant clams, sea urchins, snails with beautiful shells, crabs, rays, shrimp, sea turtles, and sharks. Every bit of space on a coral reef is taken up by some sort of living thing. And every reef is unique—no two are exactly alike.

Because of its amazing variety, the Great Barrier Reef is different things to different people. For some Australian fishermen, it is a place to make a living. The waters around the reef are filled with fish and other kinds of seafood that are very good to eat. For tourists, it is a place to play in warm water and relax on beautiful beaches. For scuba divers, it is paradise. There aren't very many places on earth where the water is so clear and where there are so many underwater wonderlands to explore.

For scientists, the Great Barrier Reef is also a place of discovery and fascination. But it is much more than that. It is a living laboratory. Researchers come from all over the world to work in this "laboratory." They come to learn about its plants and animals, its chemistry, and its history.

Scientists also are working hard to make sure that the Great Barrier Reef will have a future. Today problems like deforestation, global warming, and ocean pollution threaten to change, and maybe even destroy, fragile ecosystems like coral reefs. The

Among the many exotic animals that live on the Great Barrier Reef are nudibranchs, or sea slugs. The nudibranch shown here has fringe-like gills on its brightly colored body.

more we know about the living things that make up such a place, the better we will be able to protect them.

In the following pages, you will meet a few of the scientists who work along the "GBR." You will get an idea of the different sorts of things they are studying, the kinds of questions they are trying to answer, and the problems they have to deal with. I hope that you will also get a taste of how interesting and exciting it is to work in the incredible living laboratory known as the Great Barrier Reef.

12

THE GREATEST SHOW ON EARTH

When marine biologists Russ Babcock and Peter Harrison boarded the ferry and headed back to the mainland that day, they were very excited. During their dives around the island, they had carefully examined the corals growing just offshore. What they found convinced them that, in a just a few days, the corals were going to spawn.

Coral **spawning** is one of nature's most spectacular events. Every spring, on one or two special nights, most of the corals of the Great Barrier Reef release their reproductive cells into the water around them. Not just a few hundred, or even a few thousand, but millions of corals participate in this unforgettable event. Some people have called this mass spawning of corals "the greatest show on earth."

Up until about 10 years ago, very little was known about the way in which corals reproduce. But all that changed when a group of young graduate students studying at James Cook University in northern Queensland, Australia, decided to work together to learn more about coral reproduction. Peter Harrison and Russ Babcock were part of that group. These young scientists set up a field camp on an island along the Great Barrier Reef. They spent a lot of time underwater observing the corals that lived around the island. And eventually their months of hard work paid off. They discovered how most of the reef's corals reproduce. This discovery was a surprise to them and to the rest of the world.

Most coral polyps produce both female reproductive cells (eggs) and male reproductive cells (sperm). These two kinds of cells are formed deep inside the body of each polyp in the colony. Every spring, as the seawater flowing around the GBR warms up, the reproductive cells inside coral polyps start to change. Eggs turn from milky white to a bright color, usually pink, red, or orange, but sometimes blue, green, or even purple. Sperm develop long tails. When coral eggs and sperm change like this, scientists say they are "ripening."

Eventually, around the end of October (which is spring "down under"), the eggs and sperm are completely ripe. Inside each polyp, the ripe cells clump together to form a little round ball. Such a ball of reproductive cells is called an **egg bundle**. It is large enough to see with the naked eye.

At this point, the corals are ready to spawn. All they need now is a signal that will trigger them to release their egg bundles at the same time. What is this signal? Scientists have discovered that it is the full moon. Each year, the majority of the corals living along the Great Barrier Reef all release their reproductive cells on the third or fourth night after the full moon in late October or early November.

Once scientists figured out the connection between coral

This close-up photograph shows some of the individual polyps that make up a coral colony. Most kinds of polyps produce both male and female reproductive cells.

reproduction and the moon, they could predict when coral spawning would take place each year. Now as the time for spawning approaches each spring, people come from all over the world to see and study this remarkable event. Ships sail out to many different parts of the reef carrying researchers and loads of scientific equipment.

By the time the corals are ripe and the moon is full, the scientists are ready. Each night after the full moon, they make dives along the GBR until they can catch the corals in the act of spawning. Let's go along on one of these night dives and see what happens.

All day long, there has been a lot of excitement on the ship. Tonight is the third night after the full moon, and many of the researchers are sure that this will be *the* night. Everyone has been busy loading film into underwater cameras and video recorders, checking and rechecking lights and other equipment, and getting dive gear ready. Now the sun is low in the sky and it's time to go.

People with their equipment pile into several Zodiacs, small flat-bottomed boats with inflatable sides that the researchers use for traveling between the ship and the reef. The trip to the dive site is short, and soon our Zodiac is anchored above a big patch of coral. As the sun begins to set, the water, which is so clear and blue in the daytime, looks very dark.

Diving at night is a little scary. There are sharks and other

As the sun sets, divers begin a night dive. Wearing their scuba gear, they roll backward over the sides of a Zodiac into the dark water.

dangerous animals down there that you would never see in the dark until they were very, very close. But being able to watch the corals spawn is worth the risk. Everyone gets into scuba gear, tests flashlights, grabs equipment. Finally, each diver rolls over the side of the boat into the dark water.

At first you can't see anything but inky blackness. It's even hard to tell which way is up or down. But in a few moments, you can make out the lights of the other divers in the water around you. You follow them down through this eerie black world to the corals somewhere below.

The reef at night is a very different place than it is during the day. Most of the tropical fish have disappeared. As the sun went down, they swam into hiding places among the corals. Now most are asleep, safely hidden from the predators that roam the reef at night looking for a meal. Many kinds of marine snails that were hidden during the day are out and about now, crawling across the seafloor in search of food. So are dozens of black sea urchins with long, needle-like spines.

You swim over to a mound of coral and settle down next to it (after first making sure there are no prickly sea urchins nearby). Shining your flashlight on the coral, you take a close look at the hundreds of little polyps it contains. The scientists were right. This will be the night. Just under the surface of the polyps are small pink spots. Each spot is a little round bundle of eggs and sperm.

Now all you can do is wait with your flashlight aimed at the coral. Minutes pass and nothing happens. As you wait, you begin to wonder if a shark might be sneaking up behind you in the darkness. But then suddenly a small pink ball floats up from the surface of the coral in front of you. Then another and another. You forget all about sharks because the coral spawning has begun.

An egg bundle pops out of the mouth of a coral polyp (top). More bundles are just below the surfaces of other polyps (lower right).

All over the coral, bundles of eggs and sperm are now popping out of the mouths of the polyps. After being released, the bundles quickly float up toward the surface. In the lights of the rest of the divers, you can see that other corals are spawning too. Red, pink, and orange balls are streaming up from the different kinds of corals all around. The balls come faster and faster until you are in the middle of what looks like an upside-down snowstorm with multi-colored snow.

Left: Using a powerful light, a scientist observes a coral releasing egg bundles.
Below: Spawning corals produce an underwater "snowstorm" of colorful reproductive cells.

The scientists are busy. Some are taking videos and close-up photographs of the corals releasing their egg bundles. Others are collecting samples of these colorful little packages of eggs and sperm and sealing them inside plastic bags and and small bottles.

The weird underwater blizzard lasts nearly an hour. Then it stops almost as suddenly as it started. The corals have finished spawning. The job of reproducing is over until next year.

You and the other divers collect your gear and head back to the Zodiacs. As you reach the surface, you discover what happened to the egg bundles. After being squeezed out of the polyps' mouths, they floated to the surface, where they now form a thick layer on top of the water. If you could see them from the air, the billions of bundles would look like a pink oil slick spreading out over the surface of the sea all along the Great Barrier Reef.

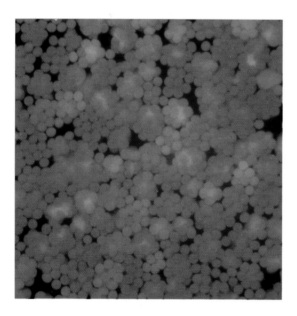

A close-up photo-graph of egg bundles floating on the surface of the water

After the bundles reach the surface, they break apart, releasing the eggs and sperm. The sperm swim off in search of other eggs. They don't join with, or **fertilize**, the eggs from their own bundles. Instead, they seek out eggs released by polyps from other coral colonies of their same species.

When a sperm cell finds the right kind of egg, the two cells join together and the egg becomes fertilized. Within a day, each fertilized egg develops into a tiny coral **larva** that drifts along with the ocean currents. After several days, the larva settles down on a reef and changes into a coral polyp. If it survives, the single polyp will grow and divide to form a new coral colony. And one day, polyps in that colony will spawn and start the cycle over again.

The mass spawning of corals on the Great Barrier Reef is a very recent discovery. There are some things about it that scientists think they understand. For example, they believe that the reason the corals spawn at night is because many of the fish that would eat coral eggs are active only during the day. At night, they are either hiding or sleeping.

Researchers think that, by spawning all together, the corals overwhelm any nighttime egg-eaters with sheer numbers of egg bundles. When the water is thick with billions of reproductive cells, only a fraction will be eaten. The majority will survive simply because there are so many in the water at the same time. For these reasons, the mass spawning of so many corals seems to make sense.

But there are other things about coral spawning that are puzzling. For example, because all the corals spawn together on this special night, the water is filled with the eggs and sperm of many different kinds of coral. How does each kind of sperm find the "right" kind of egg, one of its own species? It is pos-

This photograph shows colonies of several different kinds of coral, including staghorn and brain coral. Hundreds of species of coral release their reproductive cells at the same time during the mass spawning on the Great Barrier Reef.

sible that eggs may release special chemicals to attract the right kind of sperm, but no one has found these chemicals.

Another puzzle is why spawning takes place on just one night of the year. Limiting the important job of reproduction like this seems pretty risky. What if on the night the corals spawn, a rainstorm sweeps over the reef? Coral eggs can't survive in fresh water. Rain pouring down on the floating masses of eggs and sperm could kill them. It would be another year before the corals could try to reproduce again.

Obviously some things on the Great Barrier Reef are not as simple as they might first appear to be. Answering the questions we have about coral spawning on the reef will probably keep many scientists busy for years to come.

CHAPTER
3

SNEAKING UP
ON GIANT CLAMS

It is 2 A.M. The four members of the scientific team are fast asleep in their bunks on board the ship. Then, without warning . . . KA-CHUNG! KA-CHUNG! KA-CHUNG! The silence is shattered by the nearly deafening sound of the huge metal anchor chain being raised. Everyone is instantly awake. With a groan, they turn over and try to go back to sleep.

Having the clang of the anchor chain wake you in the middle of the night is very annoying. But it's also exciting. Why? Because it means that the ship is about to leave the dock and that this research trip out to the reef is finally underway.

The ship getting ready to leave is the R/V *Harry Messel*. R/V stands for research vessel, and this ship is one of four such vessels owned by the Australian Institute of Marine Science (AIMS, for short), which is located on the Queensland coast. The *Harry Messel* carries AIMS scientists out to study the reef for days, or even weeks, at a time. The ship is well equipped for its job. There is a laboratory, a kitchen, a galley where everyone eats, and several cabins for the crew and scientists.

Research vessels like the *Harry Messel* serve as both home and laboratory for scientists doing research on the Great Barrier Reef.

Now in the cool darkness of the spring night, the *Harry Messel* is heading out to sea. The captain sets a course that will take the ship through a maze of coral reefs to the outer (eastern) edge of the Great Barrier Reef.

The rising sun brings the ship to life, and the scientific team gathers in the galley for breakfast. Sue Williams is the young biologist in charge. She'll be assisted by Bruce, Margaret, and Rebecca (this book's author), divers who have volunteered to help Sue with her work on this trip. For the next six days, these four people will be spending a lot of time beneath the ocean's surface. They will be performing underwater "operations" on some of the reef's most remarkable animals: giant clams.

Giant clams live only on coral reefs in the Indian and Pacific oceans. There are seven different species of giant clams, and six can be found on the Great Barrier Reef. The largest species is *Tridacna gigas* (try-DAK-nuh GUY-gus). As its name suggests,

T. gigas is truly a giant. It can grow to be four and a half feet (about one and a half meters) long and three feet (about one meter) high, and weigh nearly 1,000 pounds (about 450 kilograms). None of the other species can match the huge proportions of *T. gigas*. But all of them are still much bigger than ordinary clams, like those that go into clam chowder.

Most of a giant clam's body is hidden from view between the two halves of its massive shell. Even when the shell is open, all you can usually see of the clam's soft body is its fleshy **mantle**, which stretches all the way across the shell opening. The mantles of giant clams are surprisingly beautiful. Most are decorated with spots, blotches, or stripes of brilliant colors, especially deep blues and emerald greens.

Like other kinds of clams, a giant clam continually pumps seawater through its body. There are two openings in the mantle, and water flows in through one opening and out through the other. From this stream of water, a clam filters out tiny bits of food.

Unlike all other types of clams, giant clams have a second food source. Millions of zooxanthellae live just under the surface of their mantles. Just as is the case with the coral zooxanthellae, these little one-celled plants manufacture food for their giant clam hosts. As a result, giant clams have a built-in food supply. In fact, they get so much nourishment from their "houseplants" that scientists think they may not actually need to filter food out of the surrounding water.

Although giant clams have been known to science for several hundred years, only a few researchers had studied them up until about 25 years ago. That's when people started to notice that giant clams were disappearing from coral reefs. Large numbers were being killed as food or for their shells. Suddenly, giant clams

This giant clam has a beautiful mantle of bright blue. Many small marine organisms make their homes on the clam's shell.

began to receive a lot more attention. Today many scientists are studying them, especially on the Great Barrier Reef.

Sue Williams has been working on a giant clam project for nearly a year. In her research, she is trying to find out about the relationships that exist among the giant clams that live in different parts of the GBR. She wants to know, for example, if the *Tridacna gigas* at the northern end of the reef are closely related to those living on the southern end, or whether they are just "distant cousins." She also wants to find out how the different species of giant clams are related to each other.

How can Sue answer these questions? The best way is by analyzing small pieces of the clams' mantle tissue in the laboratory. The purpose of this trip is to collect tissue samples from several different species of giant clams for Sue to use in her experiments.

After breakfast, Sue explains what everyone will soon be doing underwater. Snipping away a little piece of a clam's mantle sounds pretty simple. But the divers all know that when you're underwater, everything you do is a little bit harder and takes a little bit longer than you'd expect.

Suddenly, the *Harry Messel* cuts its engines and comes to a stop. Everyone goes out onto the deck to take a look around. They have arrived at Myrmidon, a coral reef that lies on the eastern edge of the Great Barrier Reef. All around the reef are the deep, dark-blue waters of the Coral Sea. With a roar, the heavy anchor goes rumbling down. Now it's time to go to work.

There is a fresh breeze blowing from the southeast, making whitecaps on the waves. But it is clear and sunny—a good day for diving. With the crew's help, a Zodiac is lowered into the water. The four researchers struggle into their wetsuits and load all their gear into the boat. With Sue at the motor, they head off toward the reef.

The first dive site will be in an underwater canyon in the reef nicknamed the Gutter. As the boat enters the shallow water around the reef, the color of the sea changes from dark blue to a light bluish-green. The Zodiac zooms over several "bommies," mushroom-shaped masses of coral. Sue circles the boat around

Researchers load their gear into a Zodiac in preparation for a trip to the reef.

and then cuts the engine. Slipping on a dive mask, she leans over the side and peers down into the water. "We're about half-way up the Gutter. This looks like a great spot. Let's drop the anchor here."

The four decide that Sue, Margaret, and Rebecca will dive while Bruce remains behind as the boatperson. The women strap on their weight belts, tanks, fins, and masks. Then, one by one, they roll backward over the edge of the Zodiac and disappear beneath the surface in a cloud of bubbles.

As the divers slowly descend into the underwater canyon, they stare in awe at the fairy-tale world around them. The water is incredibly clear. On the seafloor below is an enormous garden of corals growing in all shapes and sizes and colors. Jewel-like tropical fish flit here, there, and everywhere. On either side, great walls of coral rise up nearly to the water's surface.

Margaret checks her depth gauge. Six feet down . . . , ten . . . , now fifteen. She pinches her nose shut and blows to ease the pressure building up inside her ears. Down, down they all drift. Almost to the bottom now. Twenty-five feet. Gradually they come to a stop and hang, weightless, just above the seafloor. Their gauges read 32 feet (about 10 meters).

Huge *Tridacna gigas* are everywhere, their mantles spread wide between massive shells. But on this dive, Sue is after a smaller species of giant clam called *Tridacna maxima* (try-DAK-nuh MAX-ih-muh). This kind of giant clam grows about 16 inches

A scuba diver swims through an underwater canyon on the Great Barrier Reef.

29

(about 40 centimeters) long and often is found lying partly hidden among the corals. The edges of its splendidly colored mantle are iridescent and shimmer in the sunlight.

The search begins as the divers swim slowly along with Margaret in the lead. Her job is to find as many *T. maxima* as she can. After just a few seconds, she points out the first one, and Sue and Rebecca settle down to the bottom nearby. Keeping low, they move closer very slowly.

Giant clams don't have eyes like ours, but they have light- and motion-detecting sensors in their mantles. When a giant clam "sees" something big moving quickly toward it, the animal closes its shell to protect itself. And once a giant clam closes its shell, it's nearly impossible to get it open. That's why the divers must sneak up on the clams and take them by surprise.

In one hand, Rebecca holds a clam wedge, a thick triangular piece of metal. She moves closer and closer until she's about a foot from the clam. She pauses for a second, then lunges forward and sticks the wedge into the shell. The giant clam tries to snap its shell shut, but because of the wedge, it can't close up completely. There is an inch-wide gap between the two halves of the shell.

From a mesh bag they have brought down with them, Sue pulls out a forceps, a scissors, a measuring tape, and a writing slate. While Rebecca holds the wedge to keep it from slipping, Sue reaches into the gap between the shell with the forceps and grabs hold of the edge of the clam's mantle. Carefully she begins to snip out a small piece. Understandably, the clam doesn't like this very much. It tries hard to pull itself further down inside its shell. Although the procedure probably hurts a little, Sue is not really injuring the clam. It won't miss this small piece of its body, and the cut edge will heal quickly.

Sue Williams (right) takes a tissue sample from a giant clam.

Rebecca has a bundle of little plastic, zip-lock bags tucked into the glove on her left hand. Each bag is marked with a number. She takes one out, notes its number, and opens it up. (This can be pretty tricky to do underwater, especially while wearing gloves!) As Sue places the sample inside, Rebecca squeezes it down to the bottom of the little bag. Then she rolls the bag up and tucks it under the edge of her tight wetsuit sleeve.

Meanwhile, Sue has measured the clam (over the top from side to side). She points to 43 on the tape measure. Grabbing the slate and the pencil attached to it, Rebecca records the bag number (1), the species (*T. maxima*), and the clam's length (43 centimeters).

Finally, as Sue collects the tools and removes the wedge from between the clam's shell, Rebecca ties a piece of bright yellow plastic ribbon around a nearby bit of dead coral. If Sue returns to this spot on another trip to get more samples, the ribbon marker will tell her that she has already worked on this clam.

Recording observations is an important part of scientific research, whether it takes place in a laboratory or beneath the sea.

In the meantime, Margaret has found more *T. maxima* clams. She points them out, and Rebecca and Sue begin work on Clam Number 2. They follow the same procedure on this clam, and the next, and the next. But the work isn't boring because little things keep happening to make it interesting.

For example, while the team is working on Clam Number 5, a little fish with black-and-white stripes darts in and tries to snatch away the piece of tissue. Maybe it thought the divers were here to provide lunch! Clam Number 10 has such a tight grip on the clam wedge that it takes Sue nearly a minute to pry it loose. What should have been Clam Number 12 is too quick for Rebecca. It shuts up tight before she can get the wedge inside.

Every few minutes, the women check their air supply. By the

time they finish the 14th clam, all three are running low. It's time to head back. They swim along the bottom until they are directly underneath the Zodiac and then very slowly ascend.

When the divers finally break the surface, Bruce greets them with a big smile. He's glad to see them. It gets a bit boring being boatperson, sitting all alone in the Zodiac. He helps them get their tanks and weight belts into the boat, and then they clamber aboard. They haul up the anchor and return to the ship.

While the others unload the gear from the Zodiac, Sue heads to the laboratory. In the middle of the small room is a large container of liquid nitrogen. She unscrews the cap, places the bundle of samples in a sort of metal scoop, and lowers it down inside. There is a loud hissing sound as the samples freeze instantly. This is the best way to preserve them until Sue can work on them back in her laboratory at AIMS.

After a hot lunch and a short rest, everyone is ready to go again. This time they steer the Zodiac toward the other side of the reef. All afternoon, the four researchers dive around the site of an old shipwreck where there are lots of giant clams.

Around sunset, Bruce, Sue, and Rebecca go down for one last dive. They need just three more samples. The divers swim over a large sandy patch of reef, dotted here and there with *Tridacna derasa* (de-RAH-suh), the second largest species of giant clam. One of the clams looks a bit strange. It seems to be surrounded by some kind of "cloud." The three researchers swim over for a better look.

They watch patiently for a few minutes, but nothing happens. Then suddenly the clam seems to stiffen, and a fountain of white pours out through one of the openings in its mantle. The divers look at each other in amazement. The clam is spawning! It is releasing eggs into the water around it. Very few people have ever seen giant clams spawn in their natural surroundings. What an incredible bit of luck!

The light is going fast, so the divers have to hurry. Searching among the tangled corals, they find three more *T. maxima* and take tissue samples. When they are finished, Sue cups her hands together—the divers' signal for "boat." Bruce and Rebecca nod, and they all head back to the Zodiac.

Then from out of the shadows near a big mound of coral, a shark glides into view. The three divers freeze, instantly alert. The shark swims slowly by, its flat, black eyes watching, watching. . . . Then it vanishes into the shadows again. The researchers exchange glances. Swimming close together now, they waste no time in getting back to the Zodiac.

It has been a long, tiring day. But they have 30 samples of *T. maxima* mantle tissue to show for their hard work. Back in her laboratory at AIMS, Sue will extract the enzymes that each piece of tissue contains. Enzymes are special kinds of proteins that are manufactured by living cells. The DNA, or genetic material, inside each cell controls this manufacturing process. After Sue extracts the enzymes, she will perform special tests on them. The tests will show if there are any differences among the enzymes in different clams. If one clam's enzymes are different from another's, that means that their DNA is different, too. The more different the DNA, the more distantly related the two clams are.

Over the next few years, Sue hopes that she can use her research to make up a "family portrait" of giant clams on the Great Barrier Reef. She wants to be able to show which clams are related to each other, and how closely.

Other scientists who work on giant clams will find that information very useful. For example, there are several groups

Giant clams are endangered on many reefs in the South Pacific. With the help of scientists, these spectacular animals may soon be common again.

of marine biologists trying to develop ways of raising giant clams on huge "farms" in the sea. On these ocean farms, thousands of baby giant clams would be produced each year from the eggs and sperm taken from just a handful of large adult clams (called broodstock clams). The babies would be cared for until they were large enough to survive on their own. Then they would be used to replace the giant clams that have disappeared from coral reefs all over the South Pacific.

Because it is better to use broodstock clams that are distant, rather than close, relatives, Sue's findings about the relationships among the giant clams of the Great Barrier Reef will be useful to these researchers. The information will help them to select healthy adult clams that will make the best "parents" for future generations of farm-raised giant clams.

A dugong calf swimming with its mother. Attached to the female dugong's body is a suckerfish, a harmless hitchhiker.

CHAPTER
4

MERMAIDS OF THE GREAT BARRIER REEF

L ong ago, sailors traveling along the northern shores of Australia occasionally spotted what they thought were mermaids swimming near their ships. Mermaids, mysterious creatures with the upper body of a woman and a fish-like tail, were believed to live in many of the world's oceans. Today, we know there are no mermaids. So what did these sailors see? It's very likely that what they thought were "mermaids" were actually dugongs.

A dugong (DOO-gahng) is a kind of sea cow, a large marine mammal. Sea cows feed on underwater plants that grow in shallow water. They dive for their food and spend most of their time submerged, only coming to the surface to breathe. There are four kinds of sea cows in the world today: the dugong and three species of manatees (man-uh-TEES). Dugongs live in the South Pacific. Their manatee cousins are found on the other side of the world: in western Africa (the West African manatee), in South America (the Amazonian manatee), and throughout the Caribbean (the West Indian manatee). All four kinds of sea cows are considered to be endangered animals.

Dugongs grow between 7 and 11 feet long (2.2 to 3.4 meters) and weigh around 900 pounds (400 kilograms). Their bodies are shaped like torpedoes—round in the middle and tapered at either end. Dugongs have large, powerful forked tails (shaped something like a whale's tail) and two front flippers. Their massive heads end in squared-off snouts that have huge muscular upper lips covered with coarse, bristly hairs. Dugongs use their big lips to pull up bunches of seagrass, which is their favorite food.

For hundreds of years, dugongs remained almost as mysterious as the mythical mermaids. Little was known about them because they were shy and very difficult to study. But about 25 years ago, something happened along the coast of northeastern Australia that enabled scientists to find out more about the dugongs of the Great Barrier Reef.

In 1964, dead dugongs began to wash up on beaches in Townsville and several other northern Queensland cities. These were areas where shark nets had been set up offshore in order to keep sharks away from public beaches. The shark nets worked (no one has ever been attacked by a shark in Australia where shark nets are used). But now and then, dugongs would become entangled in the nets. Unable to get to the surface to breathe, they would drown. Eventually their bodies would wash up on the sand.

This unhappy situation provided a rare opportunity. Few scientists had ever had the chance to examine the body of a dugong closely. So whenever a dead dugong washed ashore, it wasn't long before someone from the dugong research program at James Cook University arrived at the scene. Dugong researchers George Heinsohn and Helene Marsh spent many hours scrutinizing every part of these unfortunate animals. They measured and weighed and probed and dissected and took lots of samples. It wasn't very pleasant work. But in doing it, they learned a lot about dugongs. For example, by analyzing what a dugong had in its stomach, the scientists could tell what kinds of seagrasses it had been eating.

Some of the most interesting new information about dugongs came from studying their teeth. Dugongs don't have many teeth. They start life with only 12 molars and lose most of those when they reach adulthood. But up near the front of their mouths, dugongs also have two special teeth called tusks that they keep throughout their lives.

Helene Marsh found dugong tusks very interesting. She cut them in half and studied the cut surface. Helene discovered that

A dugong tusk split in half to show its layers. Each layer represents one year in the animal's life. (The ruler in the corner of the photo is one centimeter in length.)

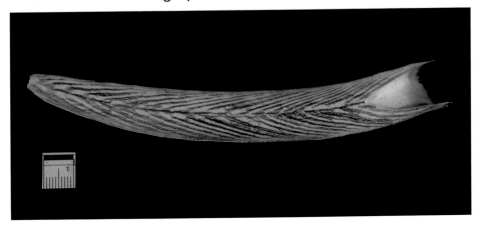

the tusks are made up of many layers. By comparing the tusks of different dugongs, from young calves to very old adults, she figured out that each layer in a tusk represents one year in a dugong's life. That was an important discovery because it meant that, by counting the layers in a tusk, you could tell how old any dugong was. After studying many tusks, Helene Marsh came to the conclusion that dugongs live 70 years or more—nearly as long as many people.

Helene Marsh's studies also revealed new information about female dugongs and their calves. Females don't start having calves until they are at least 10 years old. After that they have only one calf every 3 to 5 years. The calf takes a long time, around 13 months, to develop inside its mother's body. When it's born, it is nearly 3 feet (1 meter) long and weighs about 65 pounds (30 kilograms). Each pregnancy leaves behind a telltale scar on the inside of the mother dugong's uterus. So by counting such scars in female dugongs she examined, Helene could tell how many calves they had given birth to during their lifetimes.

By putting together information about how long dugongs live and how often females have calves, the researchers discovered an important fact. Although dugongs live a long time, they reproduce very slowly. This was disturbing news. Every year, a certain number of dugongs were legally hunted by Aboriginal people in Australia. Others died in shark nets, and still others drowned in fishermen's nets. The scientists began to wonder—were more dugongs dying each year than could be replaced by newborn calves? Was the dugong going to disappear from the Great Barrier Reef?

In order to answer these questions, the dugong researchers needed to get an idea of how many dugongs there were along the Great Barrier Reef. But how? Dugongs are hard to spot from boats, and there was an enormous amount of ocean to search. It seemed that there was only one realistic way to tackle this job: count the dugongs from the air.

It wasn't long before dugong researchers found themselves in an airplane, flying over the reef. They did have some idea where to look for dugongs. The animals spend most of their time where their food is—in beds of seagrass that grow in shallow water near the mainland and around some reefs. As dugongs eat, they sometimes leave behind a winding trail where they have munched away the seagrass and stirred up the sand. These trails can usually be seen from the air, and they were what the researchers tried to look for.

Once a group of dugongs was spotted, the plane would fly directly over it so the animals could be counted. From the air, dugongs look like fat brown logs floating on the waves. The scientists recorded the number of dugongs they saw, approximately how big each one was, the number of calves in the group, and what the dugongs were doing (feeding, swimming, or just lying idle on the surface).

Counting dugongs from airplanes turned out to be rather tricky. The biggest problem was that dugongs spend most of their time submerged. Unless the water is unusually clear and calm, they can be seen only when they come to the surface to breathe. The scientists realized that as they flew over a group of dugongs, they were seeing only some of the animals that were actually there. They couldn't tell how many more were just out of sight beneath the surface.

It was also hard to count dugong calves. When a calf is very small, it usually swims right alongside its mother or rides on her back. From the air, a mother and her calf often look like one animal.

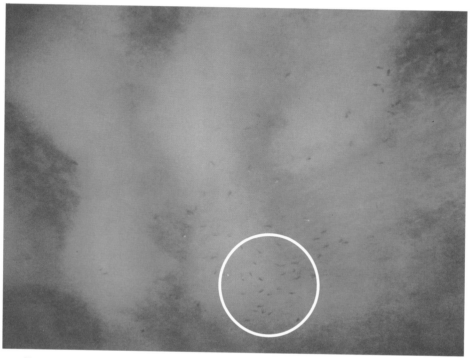

Dugongs seen from an airplane flying high above a seagrass bed

Despite these problems, the scientists were able to estimate that there are approximately 70,000 dugongs in Australian waters. Nearly 12,000 of those live along the Great Barrier Reef. That was good news because no one had thought there were that many.

But the airplane surveys gave scientists only a "big-picture" view of dugongs. They now knew approximately how many dugongs were around and where some of their feeding grounds were. But they still knew almost nothing about the habits of individual dugongs. How could they learn more?

Scientists have studied all sorts of animals, both on land and in the sea, by using radio transmitters. In most cases, an animal is captured and a small radio transmitter is attached to its body. The easiest way is to put the transmitter in a kind of collar that goes around the animal's neck. When the animal is set free, researchers can follow it wherever it goes by tracking the signal that the transmitter gives out. They can learn how far it travels and where it spends most of its time.

Helene Marsh decided to try radio-tracking dugongs, something no one had ever done before. But there was a problem—how do you attach a transmitter to a dugong? Since dugongs don't really have necks, radio collars wouldn't work. The solution to the problem came from the United States, where researchers had been radio-tracking West Indian manatees off the coast of Florida for several years. The American scientists used a floating radio-transmitter system that was secured to the manatee's tail.

Using this system as a model, Helene Marsh and her colleagues developed the first dugong radio tracker. One piece was a sort of belt that fit around the narrow part of a dugong's tail. The belt was connected to a piece of nylon rope, which in turn was attached to a floating radio transmitter. Except for the times when the dugong made a deep dive (which wasn't very often), the transmitter would bob along at the surface, trailing behind the animal wherever it went. To keep the dugong safe, the researchers designed the belt to come off if the transmitter became tangled up in something.

The next step was to capture several dugongs and attach transmitter devices to each one. To do this, Helene Marsh needed an airplane, a boat fitted out with two powerful outboard motors, nets, an inflatable stretcher, and several assistants. This is how the capture worked.

First the plane was sent out to spot dugongs. After locating some animals, the pilot sent a radio message to the boat, describing where the dugongs were, and the boat headed off in that direction.

Once the researchers in the boat located the dugongs, they singled out one particular animal. Then the chase was on. Dugongs can swim fairly fast when they want to, although they must keep coming to the surface to breathe. After being chased for a while, the dugong would eventually get tired and begin to slow down. Then the boat was maneuvered alongside the swimming animal.

Several assistants stood along the side of a boat, all holding onto a small net. When the dugong came up for its next breath, they slipped the net over its head and pulled tight. The boat was brought to a quick stop, and one assistant jumped into the water. Working fast and trying to keep clear of the thrashing dugong, the diver slipped the stretcher under the animal's body and inflated it.

In a matter of seconds, the dugong was high enough out of the water so Helene or one of her assistants could fasten the belt of the transmitter device around the animal's tail. Then the team let the air out of the stretcher and eased the dugong gently back into the water. With a flip of its tail, the animal quickly swam away, with the transmitter trailing along behind on the surface.

The transmitters that Helene and her fellow scientists made worked well. With their help, the researchers could track individual dugongs swimming around at sea while they themselves remained safe and dry on land. The floating transmitters gave off constant signals, which were picked up by weather satellites orbiting the earth. The signals were relayed back to earth, where computers calculated where the dugongs were.

44

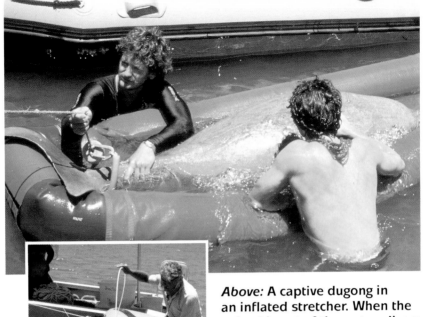

Above: **A captive dugong in an inflated stretcher. When the animal is out of the water, divers can attach the belt of a radio transmitter to its tail.** *Left:* **With the transmitter in place, the dugong is ready to be released. As it swims, the tracking device will trail behind it in the water.**

In the last few years, Helene Marsh and her coworkers have put transmitters on more than 20 dugongs. In most cases, the transmitter devices stayed on the dugongs for at least several months before they came off or stopped working. That was usually long enough to get a good idea of where the animals were spending most of their time. Based on these radio tracking experiments, it looks as if dugongs rarely wander far from their "homes" along the GBR. These homes are usually large beds of seagrass. One particular male dugong seemed to be quite a traveler, though. In one nine-week period, he made several trips between two seagrass beds that were 85 miles (140 kilometers) apart.

Helene Marsh, George Heinsohn, and other researchers have learned much about the mysterious dugong over the past 20 years or so. They now know that dugongs are not rare along the Great Barrier Reef. But they still aren't sure what effect humans, with their nets and power boats and pollution, are having on the dugong population. In fact, they think that it will take 10 more years of research before they will know for sure if the reef's dugong population is in danger.

Until then, the researchers will continue to study these fascinating animals. They would like to figure out safe ways to mark or tag individual dugongs so they could be recognized from a distance. They are also trying to get the Australian government to turn more and more seagrass beds into "dugong sanctuaries" where the dugongs will be safe from hunters and fishermen's nets. Most of all, the scientists are trying to help people realize how important it is to care about and protect the elusive "mermaids" of the Great Barrier Reef so they will never disappear.

CHAPTER 5

A Surprise at the End of a String

If you took a boat and sailed up the northeastern coast of Australia, you would be traveling between two of the most interesting places in the world. On the right side of your boat would be the islands and reefs of the Great Barrier Reef. And on your left would be mangrove forests made up of millions and millions of mangrove trees that grow right down to the water's edge.

Mangroves are tropical trees that live where land and sea come together. Few kinds of trees can grow close to the ocean's edge because salt kills most land plants. But mangroves thrive in salty places.

Some of the scientists who work along the Great Barrier Reef do their research not at sea but in the mangrove forests. Why? Because what happens in these forests affects the plants and animals that live offshore and along the reef. Let's head for land,

A mangrove forest at high tide (above) and at low tide (left). When the tide is out, the roots of the mangrove trees are exposed.

anchor our boat, and see what a mangrove forest is like.

A mangrove forest is different from any other kind of forest on earth. Right now the tide is out. The sea has drained away from around the bottoms of the trees, and their roots are exposed. Mangrove trees have some roots that grow *above* the ground. When the tide is high, these roots are covered by water. But at low tide, the trees look as if they are standing on a tangled mass of spindly legs.

48

The ground looks firm, but as you step out of the boat, you sink deep into mud. Lots of mud. Soft, gooey, black mud that smells terrible. You take another step and sink even deeper. As you lift your foot to try again, your shoe nearly stays behind in the black muck below. You will never get anywhere this way. So you do what the scientists who work in the mangroves do—you walk on the roots of the mangrove trees! It's tricky at first to keep your balance on the slippery roots and squeeze through places where the roots grow tightly together. But it's much better than walking in the mud. And from your position above the ground, you can take a good look around.

Above your head are the green, leafy tops of the mangrove trees. They are so close together that they cut out much of the sunlight, but it is still very hot and humid in the forest. Moving up and down the trunks of the trees are ants and beetles and other insects. Spiders have spun strong webs between some of the trees. Huge wasps fly in and out of a nest hanging beneath a twisted branch.

Off in the distance, you can see the dark shapes of fruit bats hanging from the branches of several trees. Fruit bats (Australians call them flying foxes) hang upside down from tree branches during the day. They are supposed to be resting. But instead they screech and squawk and squabble with each other all day long. At sunset, when the light fades from the sky, the fruit bats will fly off together in search of ripe fruit to eat.

On the ground below, small crabs are scurrying around, darting here and there across the mud beneath the tangled roots. Some keep popping in and out of the little round holes in the mud that lead to their underground burrows. When the tide comes in, the crabs will disappear down these holes. The muddy ground and the roots you are now standing on will gradually be

Many kinds of small fish find shelter among mangrove roots.
In the center of this photograph, you can see a mudskipper, an
unusual fish that climbs out of the water in search of food.

covered by seawater. With the water will come other kinds of
animals. Smooth flat rays will appear to dig for food in the soft
mud. Tiny fish will arrive by the thousands.

Mangroves are important "nurseries" for many kinds of fish
that live along the GBR. For the fragile youngsters of many
species of fish, the mangrove forest is a safe place to live until
they have grown large enough to venture out into the open sea
and the reef. When danger threatens, little fish can simply swim
into small spaces among the tangled tree roots where predators
can't get at them.

As you stand perched on the mangrove roots, you notice
something else going on in the forest. A yellow mangrove leaf
falls from a tree and drifts past your face. A moment later,
another one lands on your head. Suddenly you realize that

everywhere around you, leaves are falling from the branches of the mangrove trees. Not a lot all at once, but a few all the time. Leaves drift down steadily to land on the mud around the twisted mangrove roots.

In most forests, when leaves fall from the treetops, they collect on the ground around the bottoms of the trees. Insects and other small animals nibble at some of them, but most just rot wherever they land. With the help of decomposer organisms like bacteria and fungi, the leaves gradually fall apart and dissolve. When they do, the minerals and other nutrients that they contain soak down into the soil around the roots of the trees. Trees take up these nutrients from the soil and use them to grow and to make new leaves, flowers, fruits, and seeds. Year after year, this cycle goes on. The nutrients move from the trees to the leaves to the soil and then back to the trees again.

What happens to all the leaves that constantly rain down from the branches of the mangrove trees? A mangrove forest on the coast isn't like other kinds of forests. Twice each day, the sea flows in and out of the mangroves with the changing tides. Each time the tide goes out and the water retreats, some of the fallen leaves wash out to sea. They are gone before they have a chance to rot and return their nutrients to the forest floor.

Alistar Robertson is an Australian scientist who studies mangroves in tropical places such as the northeastern tip of Australia and Papua New Guinea. When Alistar started working along the Queensland coast (just opposite the Great Barrier Reef), he was interested in learning more about how nutrients "flow" through mangrove forests. He was especially curious about just how much of the total nutrient pool (all the nutrients available for living things to use) was escaping from the forest in the form of leaves that washed out to sea with tides.

Researcher Alistar Robertson studying decomposing mangrove leaves on the forest floor

Alistar began his research with some simple experiments that he hoped would help him discover how quickly fallen mangrove leaves can decompose in the forest. For one experiment, he collected fallen mangrove leaves and put some into mesh bags. He put the bags on the ground in places where they couldn't be washed away by the tides. Then in order to make sure that the bags weren't preventing decomposer organisms from getting at the leaves, he tied strings to a number of individual leaves and secured the other ends of the strings to mangrove roots. He left the tethered leaves lying on the muddy forest floor.

Several days later, when he came back to check on his experiment, the leaves that had been tied with strings were gone. Had the knots come undone and the strings washed away? He got down on his hands and knees to search through the mud and tangled roots. No, the strings were all there, each still securely tied to a mangrove root.

When Alistar followed the strings, he found that each one disappeared down a small hole in the mud. These holes looked like the entrances to the underground burrows of crabs. He pulled up the strings one by one. At the end of some, there was nothing but a knot. At the end of others, however, were the remains of a partly eaten leaf. Could crabs have taken the leaves underground and eaten them?

To find out, Alistar tied more leaves to strings and then simply watched and waited. It wasn't long before the "thieves" appeared. They *were* crabs! Quick-moving little crabs that popped up out of their burrows and snatched the leaves with their claws. Some of the crabs turned right around and hurried back into their burrows, pulling the leaves down behind them. Others sat on the surface and munched away for a while. Eventually they, too, disappeared down their holes, carrying the leftovers with them to finish eating in the safety of their underground homes.

The discovery of the crab thieves explained something that other scientists had noticed about the mangroves. Even at low tide, leaves never seemed to pile up on the floor of the mangrove forests, even though they were constantly drifting down from the treetops. Now it was clear why many leaves disappeared from the forest floor nearly as fast as they fell. They were being picked up and eaten by crabs such as these.

After doing some additional experiments, Alistar and other scientists learned that these little crabs play a remarkably important role in the mangrove forests. By quickly picking up fallen leaves, they limit the number of leaves that wash out to sea. Crabs collect at least a third of all the mangrove leaves that fall to the forest floor. (In some places they may collect more than two-thirds of the leaves.)

What's more, leaves carried underground rot faster than those left on the surface. And when the leaves are eaten, the nutrients they contain return to the soil especially fast, since it doesn't take long for crab wastes to decompose. Because of the crabs, nutrients that would otherwise be lost from the mangrove forest are returned to the soil so that the trees can reuse them again and again.

Leaf-eating crabs were a surprise for mangrove researchers. But such unexpected discoveries often pop up in scientific research. It is one of the things that makes research so interesting!

CHAPTER

6

THE MYSTERIOUS MOUND-BUILDERS

The moon hasn't come up yet on this late November night, so it is still very dark on the beach. Dark, but not quiet. All sorts of different sounds float out of the warm humid night. The rhythmic "whoosh-hiss" of waves as they first surge up on the beach and then slip back to sea. The eerie wailing of curlews, long-legged birds that call to one another throughout the night. The night wind sighing softly through the trees above the beach. And the muffled crunching sound made by bare feet walking through loose sand.

The feet belong to Colin Limpus and Jeff Miller, two researchers working with the Queensland National Parks and Wildlife Service. As the men make their way up the beach, they shine powerful flashlights back and forth across the sand in front of them. Suddenly the lights illuminate a small metal stake with an orange ribbon tied to its top.

As the two men move closer, they can see the shallow mound of sand marked by the stake. The mound is about four feet (1.2 meters) across. Strange tracks that look as if they were made by a wide tractor tire lead up to and away from the mound. Who or what made this mound in the sand and left behind such odd-looking tracks? And why have Jeff and Colin come to the mound in the middle of the night?

Both the tracks and the mound were made by an animal that spends nearly its entire life in the sea. On a few nights each year, however, it leaves its salt-water home and crawls out onto land. The mysterious mound-builder is a female sea turtle. The mound is a nest for her eggs.

The Great Barrier Reef is one of the few remaining places on earth where sea turtles can still be found in large numbers. It is one of the most important sea turtle habitats in the world. Six different kinds of sea turtles can be found there. The most common species are the green turtle, the hawksbill turtle, the loggerhead turtle, and the flatback turtle.

The GBR is an ideal home for sea turtles. In the maze of corals that make up the individual reefs, turtles find protection from sharks and other predators. The reefs provide them with the food they eat: algae, seagrass, marine snails, crabs, sponges, soft corals, and jellyfish. Each sea turtle has its own home feeding ground, or territory, where it may live for many years.

Beginning in October, many adult sea turtles leave their feeding grounds and migrate, often thousands of miles, to special breeding areas in other parts of the ocean. When they arrive, males court and mate with females. After mating, the males return directly to their home territories. The females, however, head off on another journey. This time their destinations are the quiet waters off the beaches where they will lay their eggs. Not just any beach will do. Even though there are countless beaches throughout the GBR and along the mainland coast

The green turtle is one of several species of sea turtles that make their homes on the Great Barrier Reef. Female sea turtles lay their eggs on the beaches of the reef's islands and along the coast.

nearby, only a special few are used by sea turtles as nesting sites.

Some species are particularly choosy about where they lay their eggs. Thousands of female green turtles, for example, nest each year on Raine Island, a tiny patch of land near the northern tip of the GBR. Raine Island is one of only a few places left in the world where green turtles nest. On certain nights during the nesting season, there are so many green turtles on the beaches of Raine Island that there is hardly room for them to move!

A female turtle that is ready to lay her eggs comes ashore after dark, usually at high tide. Cautiously leaving the water (the slightest movement or sound will scare her back in), she makes

A female flatback turtle uses her front flippers to dig a "body pit."

her way slowly up the beach. She uses her flippers to drag her heavy body through the sand. This is hard work for an animal that is designed for life in the water. It may take her many minutes to crawl up the beach to the area of loose sand that lies above the high water mark. This is where she will build her nest.

The turtle begins her nest by making a "body pit." Using her front flippers, she flings away dry loose sand until she is lying in a circular depression about 8 inches (20 centimeters) deep. When the body pit is finished, she starts on the egg chamber, the special cavity where her eggs will go. Sea turtles dig the egg chamber using only their rear flippers. The two flippers alternately dig into the sand, scoop out a "flipperful," and deposit it off to the side. Gradually the chamber gets bigger and bigger.

58

When complete, the egg chamber is shaped like a big bottle, with a short, narrow neck and a large, rounded bottom. It's hard to believe that something as awkward-looking as a flipper can dig such a perfectly shaped hole in the sand. What's even more amazing is that the turtle does all of this using only her sense of touch—she faces away from the nest the entire time.

When the chamber is just the right size, egg-laying begins. One by one, the eggs drop into the chamber. They look a lot like ping-pong balls. After all the eggs are laid, the turtle covers them with sand and packs it down with her rear flippers. Then she fills in the body pit and mounds sand up over the nest. Her job complete, she crawls back down the beach and disappears into the sea without ever looking back.

This particular night, Colin and Jeff are working on the secluded beach that lies behind the Australian Institute of Marine Science. For the past month, female flatback turtles have been coming up the beach to nest. There are now nearly 30 nests on this mile-long stretch of sand. Each one has been marked with a stake to help the researchers find them in the dark. For the next several hours, these two scientists will be examining the turtle nests and the eggs they contain. By doing so, they hope to learn more about this particular kind of sea turtle.

This first nest is quite far from the water. The two men carefully examine the tracks leading up to it. They can see the marks made by the flippers on each side of the smooth wide track created by the bottom surface of the shell as it drags through the sand. "From the look of the track, I'd say this turtle is missing part of her right rear flipper," Colin says. He makes a quick sketch of this distinctive track in his notebook and measures its width. Sea turtle tracks are like signatures left behind in the sand—no two are exactly alike.

A loggerhead turtle laying eggs

When they reach the nest, Colin and Jeff measure the width of the body pit. This information, along with the width of the track, gives them a good idea of how big the turtle was that made this nest. Kneeling down, the two men then dig into the mound with their hands. They each clear away the loose sand from a spot. Then, reaching deeper down, they feel around in the moister sand below. After a few seconds they both stop and try again in a new spot. They continue like this for almost a minute. Finally Jeff calls out, "Here it is!" His fingers have touched firmly packed sand—he has found the "neck" of the egg chamber.

Working quickly but carefully, Jeff scoops away handfuls of sand. He digs deeper and deeper, until suddenly a spot of white appears in the brown sand—a turtle egg. Very gently, he removes more sand until a half dozen eggs are exposed.

Colin places a thermometer in the sand near the uncovered eggs. Sea turtles rely on sun-warmed sand to incubate their eggs. And the temperature is very important. If the temperature inside the egg chamber is too cool, the tiny embryos inside the eggs will not develop. If the temperature is too warm, the developing turtles will be killed by the heat.

Scientists have also discovered that the temperature of the nest during the middle of the incubation period determines the sex of the baby turtles. Amazingly, temperature differences of only a few degrees will determine whether the hatchlings are all females, all males, or a mixture of both sexes.

Now Jeff gently picks up one of the eggs for a closer look. He is careful not to tip it from side to side or turn it over. Any disturbance like that can kill the fragile embryo inside. Holding the flashlight near, he peers at the egg.

Freshly laid turtle eggs have a soft, leathery shell that is translucent (you can vaguely see the structures inside). As time passes, however, the shell gradually turns very white and opaque (you can't see the structures inside at all). This change begins at the top of the egg, where a small circle of white first appears.

Each day the white circle is a little bigger, gradually spreading downward over the sides of the egg. By the time the egg is ready to hatch, it will be completely white. Turtle researchers know how quickly the eggs of each species of sea turtle turn white. So almost at a glance, Jeff and Colin can tell how old the egg is. And knowing this, they can calculate when the eggs in this nest were laid and when they will hatch.

As it turns out, the eggs in the nest are about two weeks old. It will be at least another two weeks before they are ready to hatch. When they do, the baby turtles will wriggle up through the sand and make a mad dash for the ocean. Many will be eaten by birds, lizards, and crabs. For those that make it safely into the water, there will still be many dangers, like reef fish and sharks, to avoid.

After recording a few more details about the eggs, the egg chamber, and the nest, the two men cover the eggs with sand. Then they rebuild the mound so it looks just as it did when they found it. Now they are ready to head off down the beach in search of the next nest. When they find it, they will measure and dig and check and record all over again. By sunrise they hope to have checked all the nests on this beach—that will be a good night's work!

For many biologists who study sea turtles, the Great Barrier Reef is one of the best "laboratories" in the world. Over the past 20 years, quite a bit has been learned about these elusive and endangered animals. But researchers are still looking for answers to questions such as these: Do female sea turtles return to the same beaches where they themselves were hatched to lay their

After laying her eggs, a sea turtle struggles back across the beach and returns to the sea.

eggs? Where do the baby sea turtles go once they reach the water? How do sea turtles navigate on their long-distance journeys? And what effects do we humans have on sea turtles?

With the help of scientists like Jeff and Colin, we hope that we'll be able to answer these and other questions about sea turtles one day soon. The more we know about these remarkable reptiles of the sea, the better our chances of protecting and preserving them will be.

By consulting the "diaries" of fish, researchers have learned a great deal about these colorful inhabitants of the Great Barrier Reef.

CHAPTER
7

A FISH'S DIARY

Have you ever kept a diary? Many people do. They write down in a little book everything that happens to them. Day by day, week by week, year by year, their diary becomes a record of their life.

You might be surprised to hear that fish have diaries, too. Obviously fish don't write down their experiences in little books. A fish's "diary" is actually a small bony ball, called an **otolith** (OH-tuh-lith), that lies deep inside its head.

Fish have three pairs of otoliths. They are found in the small spaces of a fish's inner ear. Otoliths seem to help fish keep their balance in the water. Without these little "earbones," fish would probably have a hard time swimming straight. Otoliths may also be important for a fish's hearing.

Some kinds of fish have small otoliths, while others have big ones. No one really knows why. But it's clear that just because a fish is large doesn't mean it will have large otoliths. For example, black marlins are very large ocean fish that have long pointed bills. But the otoliths in a 1,000-pound (450-kilogram) marlin are no bigger than the head of a pin. By comparison, red snappers (a kind of fish you may have had for dinner) are much smaller than marlins. But a red snapper may have otoliths the size of a grape.

How can an earbone buried deep inside a fish's head be a diary, a record of its life? When a fish begins life, its otoliths are very, very small. As the fish grows, however, so do its otoliths. Every day, a tiny layer of bony material is added to the outside of each one. Layer by layer, the otoliths are built up. This process continues, day after day, year after year, for as long as the fish lives. The many layers are like the pages in a diary. If you know how to read them, you can learn a surprising amount about a fish.

Tony Fowler, a biologist who studies fish on the Great Barrier Reef, sits hunched over a table in a laboratory at the Australian Institute of Marine Science. Spread out in front of him are a dozen bright yellow little fish. They are lemon damselfish, a species common on many coral reefs.

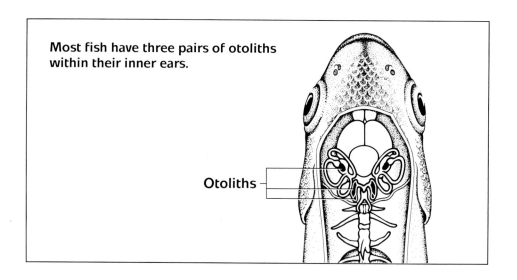

Most fish have three pairs of otoliths within their inner ears.

Otoliths

Divers stringing a net around a coral bommie in order to catch small reef fish for their research

These particular fish came from a reef near the southern tip of the Great Barrier Reef. They are part of a group of several dozen lemon damselfish that lived together on a single coral bommie. Tony and some of his fellow scientists collected these fish by stringing a huge circular net around the bommie. Then they released a chemical into the water that put the fish trapped inside the net to sleep. The fish were gathered up, weighed and measured, and then preserved in jars of alcohol.

One of the things that Tony is interested in finding out about the fish spread out in front of him is how old they are. It's hard to guess a fish's age. In fact, it's impossible to tell just by looking at it. But the otoliths of these fish contain a record that shows exactly how old each one is. Getting this information out of the tiny "diary" in a fish's head, however, is a complicated process. Let's see how it works.

The first step is to remove an otolith from the head of each fish. The otoliths of lemon damselfish look like smooth little stones that are almost clear. After washing and drying the otoliths, Tony inserts each one into a blob of soft clear plastic. The plastic dries to form a small hard block with the otolith in the middle.

When the blocks are dry, Tony uses a special grinding machine to grind away about half of each block. Then he glues the blocks—flat polished sides down—to glass microscope slides. Finally he grinds each block down from the other side until an ultra-thin "slice" of the otolith is all that's left on the slide. Such a "slice" is called a section.

A section of an otolith is much too small and thin to examine with the naked eye. Special equipment is needed to see the information recorded in it. Tony places one of the newly made slides under a powerful microscope. Connected to the microscope is a video camera. And connected to the video camera is a small computer with a video monitor (a small TV screen). The camera records what you would see if you looked through the microscope, and it displays this picture on the screen.

What does a slice of fish's otolith look like close up? To find out, take a big red onion and slice it in half down the middle. See how the onion is made up of layers? Starting in the middle, the layers look as if they are stacked one on top of the other. An

The lemon damselfish is one of the many species of damselfish that live on the Great Barrier Reef. Its otoliths look like tiny smooth stones.

otolith is a bit like an onion in that way. When it is sliced down the middle, its many layers, called rings, can be seen.

Otoliths from lemon damselfish have wide rings. Each ring starts out light and then gets darker near its outer edge. These kinds of otolith rings are called **annual rings** because each one contains all the bony material added to the otolith in one year. Because each ring represents one year, all you need to do to find out how old these lemon damselfish were is to count the annual rings in their otoliths.

Studying the image on the monitor, Tony counts the number of rings in each otolith and records the age of each fish. Even though the fish were all about the same size, they were not all the same age. Tony has found this to be true of all the lemon damselfish he collected from the bommie. Some were young, but others were much older than he expected them to be. In fact, one little fish was 17 years old!

These results are very interesting because for a long time

scientists assumed that small tropical fish living on coral reefs probably didn't live very long. Because there were so many hungry predators on the reef, they reasoned that few little fish could survive for more than a few years before being eaten. But, at least for lemon damselfish, that doesn't seem to be true. A 17-year-old lemon damselfish is proof that some small fish are very good at avoiding the dangers of the reef and can live to a ripe old age. Through their studies on the Great Barrier Reef, fish biologists like Tony Fowler are helping to change some of the ideas that scientists have had about the lifespan of small tropical fish.

But a fish's age isn't the only thing you can learn from its ear-bones. The otoliths of some kinds of fish also contain **daily rings**. As you can probably guess, daily rings are layers that form on an otolith each day. Daily rings are making it possible for scientists to answer one of the most important questions about fish that live along the Great Barrier Reef: When do they spawn? Spawning is the time when female fish lay their eggs, and a new generation begins. Scientists know that most members of each species of fish spawn at approximately the same time. But in many cases, they don't know when during the year this important event takes place.

How can daily rings in otoliths solve this mystery? Suppose you collected a fish that had such rings. By counting the rings, you would know how many days that fish had lived. Then, using a calendar, you could simply count that many days back-ward from the day the fish was caught to discover on what day its life had begun. In other words, you'd know what day its "birthday" was.

Most of the fish that make up a new generation in each species start life at about the same time. By knowing the "birthday" of

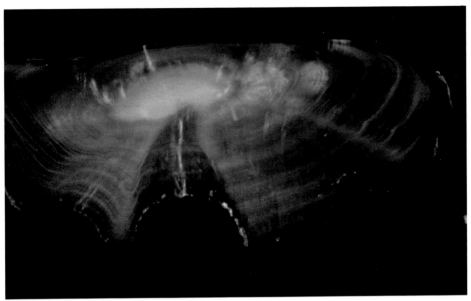

This photograph, taken through a microscope, shows a thin slice of a lemon damselfish's otolith. The rings can be clearly seen.

one fish, you'd have a very good idea when all the fish of that generation were spawned. For scientists who study fish, discovering when a species spawns each year is the first step in understanding many of the major events that take place in a fish's life.

Finally, otoliths are helping researchers learn more about who eats whom on the reef. How? There are two things about otoliths that make this possible. First of all, the otoliths of each kind of fish are unique—they are slightly different from the otoliths of all other species. An expert could look at a whole handful of different otoliths and tell you what kind of fish each one came from. Second, otoliths can't be digested. When a fish gets eaten by a predator, its body tissues are broken down in the animal's digestive tract. But not the otoliths.

Blue pullers, seen here among the branches of staghorn coral, are another species of reef damselfish. Scientists have learned about the life histories of such small tropical fish by studying their otoliths.

Because of this, researchers can use otoliths to figure out what's on the menu of animals like sharks, squids, and moray eels. Any otoliths they find in the stomachs or intestines of a fish-eating animal like a shark can be identified so the researchers will know what fish the shark has recently eaten.

Who would have thought that so much could be learned from the tiny little bones in a fish's ear?

72

CHAPTER
8

WHY THERE ARE NO SUNBURNED CORALS

At some time or another, most people have gotten sunburned. If you're out in the sun long enough, your skin turns first pink, then red. Eventually it may even begin to blister. Some sunburns are so serious that they require a trip to the hospital.

What is it about sunlight that causes our skin to burn? Actually, the light that we see coming from the sun is not the problem. Sunburn is caused by ultraviolet radiation, an invisible part of sunlight. Ultraviolet radiation, or UV light, as it is often called, is a powerful form of energy. And just as it can burn our skin, it can also harm the tissues of many other living things.

Imagine being out on a coral reef somewhere along the Great Barrier Reef at noon on a cloudless summer day. The hot tropical sun is directly overhead, beating down on you. Unless your skin is protected, it won't take long for you to begin to burn. But look down into the water, at all the corals that lie just under the surface. You would think that this intense sunlight, with the UV radiation it

A coral reef at low tide. Although the coral polyps are exposed to the ultraviolet rays of the sun, their delicate tissues are unharmed.

contains, would hurt the corals. They are very delicate animals, with nearly transparent "skin" that is even more sensitive than yours. So why aren't they getting sunburned?

For a long time, scientists believed that ultraviolet light could penetrate water no more than a few inches. So they didn't think that it was a problem for the ocean's inhabitants, even for those that lived in very shallow water. But this long-held belief turned out not to be true. UV light *does* travel through water. The clearer the water, the farther down it can penetrate. Along much of the Great Barrier Reef, where the water is very clear, the powerful rays of ultraviolet light coming from the sun can reach nearly 60 feet (20 meters) below the surface.

But are we sure UV light really harms things that live under-water in the way that it damages human skin? Paul Jokiel, a scientist working on coral reefs in Hawaii, carried out a clever experiment to show just how damaging UV light can be. He collected a variety of shallow-water reef animals that normally live in the shadows and crevices of reefs, where they are out of direct sunlight. He put these animals in a large aquarium in full sun and kept fresh seawater flowing through it all the time. Conditions inside the tank were just like those out on the reef. But then he covered one half of the tank with a sheet of clear plastic. The plastic let in the sunshine but blocked the UV rays. The other side of the tank was exposed to the full sun, UV and all.

All the animals in the plastic-covered side of the aquarium were not harmed—they were shielded from the UV rays. But all the animals that were in full sun (and exposed to UV) died within a day or two. Some died very quickly. Others lost an outer layer of "skin" first, which peeled off like a person's skin does after being badly sunburned.

This experiment proved that UV light does indeed penetrate down into seawater and that it is powerful enough to kill most marine organisms that are not protected from it in some way. The animals that Paul Jokiel used in his experiment avoid UV rays out on the reef by living in the shadows. Different reef inhabitants keep themselves safe from UV rays in other ways. For example, when the sun is high in the sky, many kinds of fish swim down into deep water where UV rays cannot reach.

But what about the corals? They can't hide in the shadows and they can't move to deeper water. Obviously they must be able to protect themselves from the deadly UV rays in some way, or they would be killed. What is their secret?

The secret to UV protection in corals lies in their tissues. Marine biologists working along the Great Barrier Reef collected samples of many different kinds of coral, from big rounded types to delicate branching varieties. Back in the laboratory, they ground up the samples and analyzed the chemicals that were in the tissues of the polyps. What they found was that corals have an unusual substance in their tissues that actually absorbs ultraviolet light.

Originally, this UV-absorbing substance was simply called S-320. No one knew very much about it. Then, as more studies were done, scientists found that not all corals contain the same amount of S-320. Corals that live in shallow water, where they are exposed to very high levels of UV light, have large amounts of S-320 in their tissues. Those that live deeper have less. Corals that live 60 feet (20 meters) or more below the surface, where only a few UV rays can reach, have just a trace. So it seems that the amount of S-320 any coral contains depends on the amount of ultraviolet light it is exposed to.

Recently, Bruce Chalker, Walter Dunlap, David Barnes, and W. M. Bandaranayake, all scientists working at the Australian Institute of Marine Science, took a closer look at the mysterious substance S-320. They collected samples of a particular kind of staghorn coral, *Acropora formosa*, which grows in many places along the Great Barrier Reef, and extracted S-320 from its tissues.

By running a series of complex laboratory tests, they found that S-320 from these corals is made up of a combination of closely related chemicals that each absorb UV light. Like the plastic sheet over the aquarium, these chemicals work together to block harmful UV rays from penetrating the tissues of coral animals. In short, they are a natural, built-in sunscreen for corals.

It didn't take the AIMS researchers long to realize that if these

Corals that grows in deep water contain smaller amounts of sunscreen chemicals than corals that live near the surface.

chemicals worked as a sunscreen for corals, they might also work for people. With the help of an Australian company, the scientists are trying to develop a new sunscreen lotion that contains the same UV-absorbing chemicals found in corals. They expect it to be much better than any sunscreen available today.

The sunscreens that you can currently buy contain substances like PABA (para-aminobenzoic acid). PABA blocks most of the UV rays that can burn the surface of your skin, but not necessarily those that can cause skin cancer. What's more, in high doses, most sunscreen substances can actually be harmful. Many people are allergic to even low doses of PABA. That is one reason why most sunscreens that use PABA have a maximum SPF of about 25.

SPF stands for "sun protection factor." The number indicates

W. M. Bandaranayake is one of the AIMS scientists studying coral sunscreens in the laboratory.

how much protection a sunscreen will give you from the sun. The higher the number, the greater the protection. If more PABA were used to increase the SPF beyond 25, however, the sunscreen itself would probably do you more harm than the UV rays you were trying to block out.

The chemicals that act as sunscreens in corals block out both the kinds of UV rays that burn skin *and* those that can cause skin cancer. And they are not toxic to people. The new sunscreen made from the components of S-320 will have a SPF of at least 50.

Australians have the highest rate of skin cancer in the world. So it seems fitting that this revolutionary new sunscreen would be developed in their country. Right now it is still in the testing stage. But if all goes as planned, it should be for sale in stores by 1994. Imagine . . . one day in the not-too-distant future, you might be protecting your skin with the same chemicals that corals on the Great Barrier Reef use to protect theirs!

In the future, this snorkler may be protected from sunburn by the same chemicals that protect the reef's corals.

A crown-of-thorns starfish feeding on coral polyps. These large starfish have caused great damage to the corals of the Great Barrier Reef.

CHAPTER
9

A CORAL-EATING STARFISH

Green Island is one of the prettiest islands on the Great Barrier Reef. It is covered with palm trees and other tropical plants. And it *used* to be surrounded by beautiful coral reefs. But in 1962, an army of destructive animals appeared on the reefs around Green Island. Hundreds of thousands of crown-of-thorns starfish seemed to come from nowhere. They moved slowly over the beautiful corals, eating the coral polyps. Many months later, the starfish disappeared as mysteriously as they had come. But the reef around Green Island wasn't beautiful anymore. It was a dreary graveyard of coral skeletons.

Not long afterward, similar armies of these starfish appeared on other reefs along the GBR. In each place the story was the same. The starfish came in great numbers, ate up most of the corals, and then disappeared. People began to worry. In just months, these starfish could destroy a reef that the corals had taken hundreds of years to build. What was happening? Would these starfish destroy the entire Great Barrier Reef?

The crown-of-thorns starfish (*Acanthaster planci*) may be the best-studied animal on the Great Barrier Reef. For more than 20 years, scientists have been investigating this unusual starfish, hoping to learn why, every now and then, it appears in huge numbers on the reef. Most people are no longer worried that we might lose the entire Great Barrier Reef to these coral-eaters. But they are still concerned about the damage that the starfish can do.

Each time there is another population explosion, or "outbreak," of crown of thorns, several square miles of coral are destroyed. And although reefs can recover from such an attack, the healing process is very slow. It may take 15 to 20 years for new corals to grow and for fish and other reef creatures to return.

After 20 years of research, what do scientists know about the crown-of-thorns starfish? For one thing, they know it is a normal reef inhabitant. In other words, it wouldn't be unusual to find a few of these starfish on any tropical coral reef in the Pacific and Indian oceans. But the crown of thorns isn't your average starfish.

First of all, it is BIG. An average-sized adult crown of thorns measures over a foot (0.3 meters) in diameter. A really large one could be more than twice that size. Most starfish have just 5 arms radiating out from a central body (called the central disk). But a crown of thorns has anywhere from 7 to 23 arms. Like all starfish, a crown of thorns uses suction-cup-like tube feet on the undersides of its arms to pull itself along. But it moves faster than other kinds of starfish, perhaps because it has so many arms.

The crown of thorns has some other unusual features. Its entire top surface is covered with long, sharp, poisonous spines. (The crown of thorns is the only poisonous starfish in the world.) Just touching the spines is painful. If you really get jabbed by

Two scuba divers take a close look at a crown-of-thorns starfish.

one, you'll end up with a wound that heals very slowly and hurts for weeks.

All starfish have mouths located on the underside of their bodies, in the middle of their central disks. To eat, a starfish pushes its stomach out of its mouth so that it comes into contact with, and then digests, its meal. But the crown-of-thorns starfish seems to do everything in a bigger-than-average way. It has an absolutely enormous stomach that it can push far out of its mouth.

When a crown of thorns feeds, it crawls onto a piece of coral and spreads its massive stomach out over a large area. Digestive juices pour out of the stomach onto the coral polyps, turning them into "coral soup." A crown-of-thorns starfish can even eat branched corals. Because its body is very flexible, it simply wraps

A crown of thorns feeding on a staghorn coral. The starfish's extended stomach can be seen in the center of the picture. The animal has already eaten the polyps in the branch on the left, leaving behind a white feeding scar.

itself (and its stomach) around the branches and eats every polyp that its stomach touches.

When the starfish is finished with its meal, it pulls in its stomach (along with the dissolved coral) and moves on, leaving behind a white patch of bare coral skeleton. These patches are called feeding scars.

While the crown of thorns eats many kinds of corals, only a few things can eat it. Probably the best known predator is the giant triton, a large marine snail. It flips the starfish over and attacks its soft underparts. But tritons are quite rare, so for the most part, the crown of thorns has few enemies.

Probably the most remarkable thing about the crown-of-thorns starfish is the number of eggs a female can produce. Every year, an average-size female releases about 60 million eggs during the spawning season. That's a lot more than other starfish produce (and most other kinds of reef creatures, too). Fertilized eggs develop into strange-looking larvae (LAR-vee) that scientists think can drift through the ocean for a long time. Eventually, larvae settle down somewhere and change into tiny starfish.

Once scientists figured out the basics about the crown-of-thorns starfish, they started to work on the details. But it hasn't been easy. In every stage of its life, the crown of thorns is a difficult animal to study. The larvae, for example, are microscopic and nearly transparent. How do you follow something like that through the ocean?

Some researchers have tried to track the larvae by scattering waterproof cards on the ocean surface above a place on the reef where adult starfish are spawning. By following the floating cards, which are easy to see, they can get some idea of where the drifting larvae might be headed. But these experiments don't really tell us much about how long the larvae can drift or where they eventually settle down.

Studying very young crown of thorns has been nearly impossible. They are only a few inches across, and they blend in perfectly with their surroundings. And you can imagine how many places there are on a coral reef where such small animals can hide. Even scientists who study them can seldom spot very young crown-of-thorns starfish out on a reef. What these youngsters do and where they go during this part of their lives remains a mystery.

Trying to study the adult starfish out on the reef has been frustrating, too. The best way to learn about an animal's habits is to track one or several individuals and see what they do and where they go over a period of time. But scientists have had a terrible time trying to track adult crown-of-thorns starfish. So far, every kind of tagging or marking system they have tried has failed. The starfish have managed to quickly get rid of dyes, harnesses, plastic tags, clipped or painted spines, nylon loops around their arms, and even stainless steel wires run through their middles!

Until scientists can figure out a way to follow the movements of adult crown of thorns, they won't be able to figure out where the armies of starfish come from when they appear on a reef. They will also be unable to discover where the starfish go at the end of an outbreak.

Some studies on crown-of-thorns starfish are done in laboratories. For this research, scientists need to collect starfish from out on the reef and bring them back alive. Even that is a tricky job. How do you pick up a big, heavy starfish that is bristling with poisonous spines? Since the spines are strong enough to puncture even heavy leather gloves, divers can't use their hands.

One team of investigators has come up with a pretty good solution. They designed a tool for picking up a crown of thorns that looks like a giant barbecue tongs. With it divers can pull the starfish off the corals and collect them underwater without having to worry about keeping their hands clear of the nasty spines.

Even though there is still much to learn about the crown-of-thorns starfish, scientists now have at least a few ideas about what might cause their population explosions. The larvae are probably the key to the outbreaks. Although a female crown-of-thorns starfish releases 60 million eggs when she spawns, normally only a few of those eggs survive and develop into adults. But imagine what would happen if *more* than the normal number of larvae survived? Even a very small increase would make a big difference. For example, just a one percent increase in the survival rate of 60 million eggs would mean an extra 600,000 starfish!

Because of their sharp, poisonous spines (above), crown-of-thorns starfish are very difficult to handle. Researchers usually use tongs to pick up the prickly animals (right).

Scientists think that, now and then, something happens in the sea or on the reefs that makes it possible for more crown-of-thorns larvae to survive than would normally. Perhaps it is even something that people do. For instance, some researchers think that fishing and shell-collecting may be destroying some of the starfishes' natural enemies.

Other scientists are looking into different explanations. What everyone wants to know is whether or not the outbreaks are occurring more and more frequently. If researchers discover that they are, then it will become all the more important to find a solution to the problem as quickly as possible. A coral reef can usually survive one attack by hordes of crown-of-thorns starfish. But if the attacks start to come on a regular basis, the reefs would not have a chance to recover. Then the Great Barrier Reef could be in real trouble.

The crown-of-thorns problem is very complicated. And it doesn't look as if answers and solutions are going to be easy to find. But research on this fascinating, mysterious, and important animal continues all along the Great Barrier Reef.

How About You?

How about you? Would you like to work in the living laboratory of the Great Barrier Reef? Be one of the people who discover where baby sea turtles go, how coral eggs and sperm sort themselves out in the water, how to help endangered marine animals like dugongs and giant clams?

Then you should think about becoming a marine biologist. Most of the scientists you have read about in this book are marine biologists. And even though they all work along the Great Barrier Reef, you have seen that they are studying many very different kinds of things.

If you are interested in science, but don't think that marine biology is the field for you, you have a lot of other options. There are many different areas of science and kinds of scientists. For example, botanists study plants. Ecologists study the way in which living things interact with their environment. Entomologists study insects, and herpetologists study snakes. There are also dozens of other kinds of scientists who are interested in everything from how the weather works to what is beyond our solar system.

Working in the living laboratory of the Great Barrier Reef, this scientist is setting up equipment to measure the amount of oxygen used by coral polyps.

Most areas of science have their own special kind of "living laboratory" too. There are rainforests, deserts, frozen polar regions, the deep sea, mountain peaks and river valleys, forests, wetlands, the atmosphere . . . the list is practically endless.

If you're thinking about becoming a scientist—any kind of scientist—here are a few suggestions that may help you along the way. First of all, make science your goal and don't let anyone discourage you from pursuing it. Read books about science.

90

Learn as much as you can about the animals, plants, and other living things that share our world and about how things work on our planet.

If you are in school, take as many science classes as you can. Work hard in your math classes because most scientists have to use math in their work. Practice writing whenever you can—scientists need to be able to write clear explanations of their discoveries. Read articles in magazines and newspapers to find out what scientists are doing today, and what they hope to do in the future.

We already know a lot about our world, but there is and probably always will be a great deal more waiting to be discovered. Science is the key to becoming part of the discoveries yet to be made.

Glossary

annual rings—layers in a fish's otoliths each of which represents one year in the animal's life

daily rings—layers in the otoliths of some fish each of which represents a day in the fish's life

egg bundle—a small ball of reproductive cells released by spawning coral polyps. An egg bundle usually includes both female egg cells and male sperm.

fertilize—to bring together a male sperm and female egg cell

larva—an animal in an immature stage of development. Both coral polyps and starfish, as well as many other kinds of marine animals, go through a larval stage before becoming adults. The plural form of the word is **larvae.**

mangroves—tropical trees that grow in an area where land and sea come together. Many mangroves have roots that grow above the ground.

mantle—the part of a giant clam's soft body that lines its shell and that can be seen when the shell is open

otolith—a small ball of bony material found in a fish's inner ear. A fish's three pairs of otoliths seem to help in keeping its balance in the water. Otoliths also contain important clues about a fish's age.

polyps—tiny individual coral animals that create coral reefs. Related to sea anemones and jellyfish, a coral polyp has a tube-like body with a mouth at one end surrounded by tentacles.

Polyps manufacture a stony material that encloses and protects their soft bodies. When the animals die, this material remains behind and eventually builds up to form coral reefs.

reefs—stony structures formed by the skeletons of thousands of coral polyps. Coral reefs are home to a remarkable variety of marine plants and animals.

spawning—the act of releasing reproductive cells, usually in water

zooxanthellae—one-celled plants that live inside the bodies of coral polyps and giant clams. Zooxanthellae use sunlight to produce food for themselves and their hosts.

Index

94

Acknowledgments The photographs and illustrations in this book are reproduced through the courtesy of: p. 2, Minneapolis Public Library and Information Center; pp. 6, 10, 12, 26, 35, 57, 60, 63, 64, 69, 72, 79, 83, 84, Great Barrier Reef Marine Park Authority; pp. 7, 9, 13, 23, 37, 47, 55, 65, 73, 81, 89, Darren Erickson; pp. 8, 66, Laura Westlund; pp. 15, 29, John Clifton; pp. 16, 19 (top), 22, 24, 28, 31, 32, 48 (top), 52, 67, 71, 74, 78, 80, 87 (bottom), 88, 90, 93, 96, Australian Institute of Marine Science; pp. 18, 19 (bottom), 20, Peter Harrison; pp. 31, 32, Australian Centre for International Agricultural Research; p. 36, Geoff Taylor; p. 58, Jiri Lochman; p. 39, Helene Marsh; p. 42, Tony Preen; p. 45, Galen B. Rathbun, U. S. Fish and Wildlife Service; pp. 48 (inset), 50, Rebecca L. Johnson; p. 77, Australian Tourist Commission; p. 87 (top), Mike Cuthill